This book is dedicated to my daughters

Thank you for being my greatest teachers

When I was a girl I would dream of sailing the seas, make dinosaur discoveries, and flying on the trapeze

The dream I wanted most to come true was to be a Mommy to the two of you

We would play in the park until it got dark

We would dance and sing
We would swing on swings

Never in a hurry

Never have a worry

I would be the best Mommy

in the whole wide world

But being a grownup isn't always fun

All I want to do is

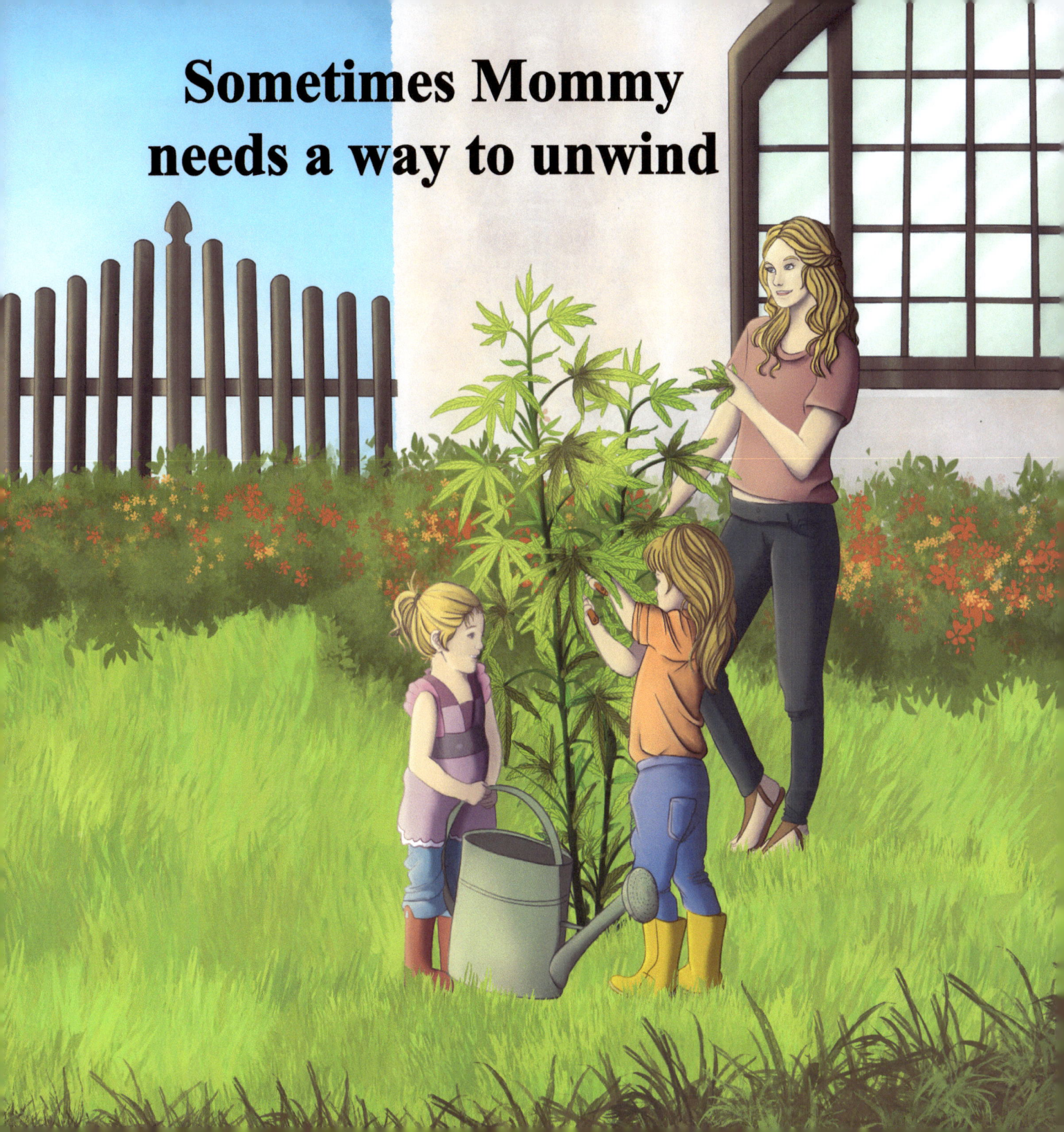

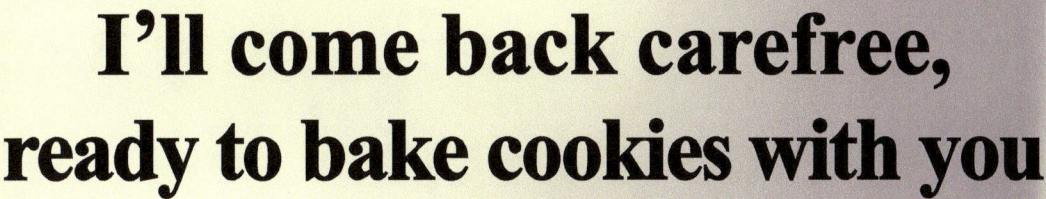

I'll come back carefree, ready to bake cookies with you

Although I may smell a little funny, I'll be a much happier Mommy

Making a mess, running around the house, building forts on the couch

Sometimes I feel like I'm going to cry

But, there are no big deals

when Mommy is high

The End

Finally a children's book to explain why some parents choose to use marijuana as a way to relax and connect with their kids. For years, this natural stress reducer has been unfairly demonized.

In writing "Why Mommy Gets High" my goal was to start a conversation between parents and their children in hopes of taking away the fear that some adults feel who responsibly use cannabis. Just as many parents choose to have a glass of wine in order to relax after a long day, marijuana when used responsibly should be viewed similarly.

"Why Mommy Gets High", explains to children that marijuana used in moderation by adults is not some scary evil substance, but rather a potentialy wonderful aid in helping parents to relax, connect, and enjoy their children.

Wendy Brazill lives in Santa Monica, CA. with her husband Chad Einbinder, they have a blended family with 6 thriving adult children. Wendy continues to paint, surf and get high.

Daniela Teichmann lives in Augsburg, Germany. She works as Video Game Developer, Children's book Illustrator and Character Designer. She is a plantparent and cat mom. When she is not working she spends her time singing, playing guitar, piano and her favorite video games.

DISCLAIMER:
The publisher and the author are providing this book and its contents on an "as is" basis and make no representations or warranties of any kind with respect to this book or its contents. The publisher and the author disclaim all such representations and warranties, including but not limited to warranties of healthcare for a particular purpose. All the information provided within is for general information purposes only and is the expressly the opinion of the author and not others. The publisher and the author are not providing any medical, legal, or other advice, professional or otherwise. The publisher and author are explicitly not encouraging the use of any medical or recreational substances, including but not limited to cannabis and related products. Any use should be consistent with applicable laws. Parents are encouraged to review the contents of this book and determine whether it is suitable for children.

www.ingramcontent.com/pod-product-compliance
Lightning Source LLC
LaVergne TN
LVHW072118070426
835510LV00003B/117